How CIOs Can Bring Business And IT Together

How CIOs Can Use Their Technical Skills To Help Their Company Solve Real-World Business Problems

"Practical, proven techniques that will show you how to use technology to make your company more successful"

Dr. Jim Anderson

Published by:
Blue Elephant Consulting
Tampa, Florida

Printed in the United States of America

Library of Congress Control Number: 2017901490

ISBN-13: 978-1542863612
ISBN-10: 1542863619

Warning – Disclaimer

Recent Books By
The Author

Product Management

- Managing Your Product Manager Career: How Product Managers Can Find And Succeed In The Right Job

- How Product Managers Can Sell More Of Their Product: Tips & Techniques For Product Managers To Better Understand How To Sell Their Product

Public Speaking

- Creating Speeches That Work: How To Create A Speech That Will Make Your Message Be Remembered Forever!

- How To Organize A Speech In Order To Make Your Point: How to put together a speech that will capture and hold your audience's attention

CIO Skills

- New IT Technology Issues Facing CIOs: How CIOs Can Stay On Top Of The Changes In The Technology That Powers The Company

- Keeping The Barbarians Out: How CIOs Can Secure Their Department and Company: Tips And Techniques For

CIOs To Use In Order To Secure Both Their IT
Department And Their Company

IT Manager Skills

- How IT Managers Can Use New Technology To Meet
  Today's IT Challenges: Technologies That IT Managers
  Can Use In Order to Make Their Teams More Productive

- How To Build High Performance IT Teams: Tips And
  Techniques That IT Managers Can Use In Order To
  Develop Productive Teams

Negotiating

- Getting What You Want In A Negotiation By Learning
  How To Signal: How To Develop The Skill Of Effective
  Signaling In A Negotiation In Order To Get The Best
  Possible Outcome

- Exploring How To Get The Deal That You Want In A
  Negotiation: How To Develop The Skill Of Exploring
  What Is Possible In A Negotiation In Order To Reach The
  Best Possible Deal

Miscellaneous

- How To Heal A Broken Leg – Fast!: Understanding how
  to deal with a broken leg in order to start walking again
  quickly

- How Software Defined Networking (SDN) Is Going To Change Your World Forever: The Revolution In Network Design And How It Affects

Note: See a complete list of books by Dr. Jim Anderson at the back of this book.

Acknowledgements

Any book like this one is the result of years of real-world work experience. In my over 25 years of working for 7 different firms, I have met countless fantastic people and I've been mentored by some truly exceptional ones. Although I've probably forgotten some of the people who made me the person that I am today, here is my attempt to finally give them the recognition that they so truly deserve:

- Thomas P. Anderson
- Art Puett
- Bobbi Marshall
- Bob Boggs

Dr. Jim Anderson

This book is dedicated to my family: Lori, Maddie, Nick, and Ben. None of this would have been possible without their constant love and support.

Thanks for always believing in me and providing me with the strength to always be willing to go out there and be my best for you.

Blue
Elephant
Consulting
Speaking. Negotiating. Managing. Marketing.

Table Of Contents

Bringing The Worlds Of Business And IT Together

As the world has become more and more digital, the importance of the role of a CIO within a firm has increased. No longer can CIOs be content to focus exclusively on technical topics. Instead, we now have to consider what the company's goals are and how technology can be used to help the company achieve those goals.

In order for both a CIO and an IT department to be successful, they are going to have to have the attention of the company's upper management. Getting that attention and then holding on to it is the job of the CIO. If you can get the attention that you need, then you'll have a much better chance of being able to secure the funding that your IT department is going to need in order to implement its programs.

Once you've been able to secure the funding that your department needs the hard work really begins. You are going to have to find ways to maximize the value that you'll be able to get out of the funding that has been allocated to you. One way to make this happen is to attempt to align what the IT department is doing with what the rest of the company is doing. Easy to say, hard to do.

One of the daily jobs of any IT department is to work with the rest of the company in order to better understand how they go about doing their jobs. This knowledge can then be used to identify new products that the IT department can create in order to simplify tasks that the company has to perform.

The tasks that an IT department performs at any given company are often quite similar. This means that the CIO would like to know what the industry best practices are. Traditionally, ITIL has been the standard definition of how to run an IT department. However, times are changing and now BDIM is starting to emerge on the scene.

At the end of the day, a CIO is going to be evaluated based on how well he or she is able to bring the business and IT together. In order to determine how well you've been able to do this, you are going to have to get comfortable with how to measure the revenue value of your company's IT department.

For more information on what it takes to be a great CIO, check out my blog, The Accidental Successful CIO, at:

www.TheAccidentalSuccessfulCIO.com

Good luck!

-    Dr. Jim Anderson

About The Author

I must confess that I never set out to be a CIO. When I went to school, I studied Computer Science and thought that I'd get a nice job programming and that would be that. Well, at least part of that plan worked out!

My first job was working for Boeing on their F/A-18 fighter jet program. I spent my days programming fighter jet software in assembly language and I loved it. The U.S. government decided to save some money and went looking for other countries to sell this plane to. This put me into an unfamiliar role: I started to meet with foreign military officials and I ended up having to manage groups of engineers who were working on international projects.

Time moved on and so did I. I found myself working for Siemens, the big German telecommunications company. They were making phone switches and selling them to the seven U.S. phone companies. The problem was that the switches were too complicated. Customers couldn't tell the difference between one complicated phone switch from another complicated phone switch. Once again I found myself working with the sales and marketing teams to find ways to make the great technology that the engineers had developed understandable to both internal and external customers.

I've spent over 25 years working as a senior IT professional for both big companies and startups. This has given me an opportunity to learn what it takes to manage an IT department in ways that allow it to maximize its output while becoming a valuable part of the overall company.

I now live in Tampa Florida where I spend my time managing my consulting business, Blue Elephant Consulting, teaching college courses at the University of South Florida, and traveling to work with companies like yours to share the knowledge that I have about how to create and manage successful IT departments.

I'm always available to answer questions and I can be reached at:

Dr. Jim Anderson
Blue Elephant Consulting
Email: jim@BlueElephantConsulting.com
Facebook: http://goo.gl/1TVoK
Web: **www.BlueElephantConsulting.com**

"Unforgettable communication skills that will set your ideas free..."

Create IT Departments That Are Productive And A Valuable Asset To The Rest Of The Company !

Dr. Jim Anderson is available to provide training and coaching on the topics that are the most important to people who have to manage IT departments: how can I build a productive IT department (and keep it together) while at the same time providing the rest of the company with the IT services that they need?

Dr. Anderson believes that in order to both learn and remember what he says, speakers need to laugh. Each one of his speeches is full of fun and humor so that what he says "sticks" with everyone.

Dr. Anderson's CIO Skills Training Includes:

1. How to identify and attract the right type of IT workers to your IT department.
2. How to build relationships with the company's senior management in order to get the support that you need?
3. How to stay on top of changing technology and security issues so that you never get surprised?

Dr. Jim Anderson works with over 100 customers per year. To invite Dr. Anderson to work with you, contact him at:

Phone: 813-418-6970 or
Email: jim@BlueElephantConsulting.com

Blue
Elephant
Consulting
Speaking. Negotiating. Managing. Marketing.

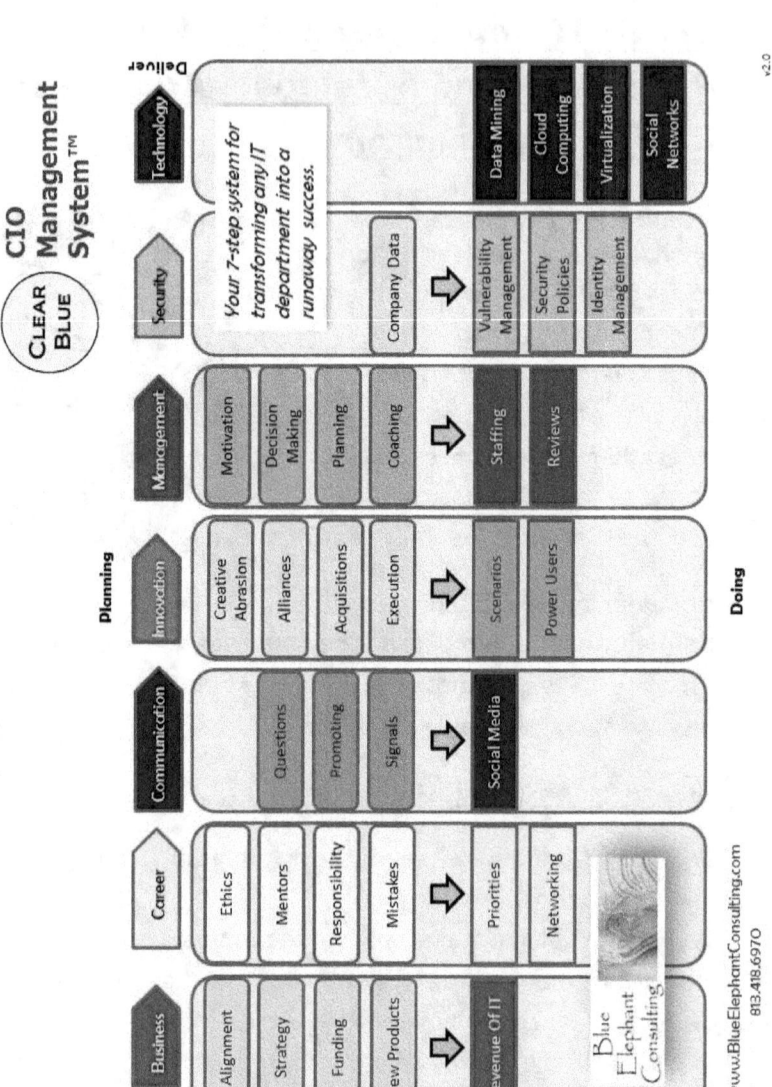

The **Clear Blue CIO Management System™** has been created to provide CIOs and senior IT managers with a clear roadmap for how to manage an IT department. This system shows CIOs what needs to be done and in what order to do it.

Chapter 1

Getting & Keeping IT Top Management's Attention

Chapter 1: Getting & Keeping IT Top Management's Attention

In my humble opinion, one of the key contributors to why so many IT projects fail is because of simple neglect. I guess the best analogy is if you were starting to drive down a highway road. When you started driving, you'd keep your hands on the steering wheel and make sure that the car was going in the correct direction and that it stayed on the road. However, if later on you took both of your hands off of the wheel, then the car would start to drift and would eventually plunge off of the road.

IT projects seem to follow this same path: when they are kicked off, everyone, including senior IT management, seems to have their hands on the steering wheel. However, as the days, weeks, months go on it sure seems like nobody is holding on to the wheel anymore and the project tends to start to drift. All too often, more people are then thrown at the project or, worse yet, the schedule is reduced which causes the project to speed up. This just makes the eventual crash all that more spectacular.

So none of this discussion is news to us IT folks – we've seen it over and over again. What we need to find is a way to stop this from happening. Jesper Simonsen is a European professor who has spent some time studying this problem. He's come up with some suggestions as to how we can go about fixing it.

Simonsen believes that the key to getting senior IT management involved in a project is to use participatory design so that they feel that they have contributed to the solution. The specific technique that he believes can be used to make this happen is called "problem mapping".

Too many IT staffers solve problems by sitting in their cubes and dreaming up new ways to deal with old problems. Participatory design requires IT staffers to deal with a problem directly. They share their views on the problem and then they offer their suggestions as to how IT can be used to solve the problem.

In order to engage senior IT management, they need to be involved in this development of an answer to why IT needs to be involved in solving the problem. This is where problem mapping comes in.

Problem mapping is designed to allow the argument regarding if and how IT should be used to solve a problem to be evaluated. It provides a means by which the argument can be visualized and helps in seeing the structure of the argument.

When you use problem mapping, you create a table that has four columns with the following headers:

- Problem / Need
- Causes
- Consequences
- Solutions

The real power of using a problem map is that it will force all involved to talk about what they see as being the real problem. The link between what they are proposing as a solution and the original problem is very clearly shown.

The key point to make here is that by making the whole problem solving process so visible, you will actively engage the top management in the process. They will be given an opportunity to sit back and challenge, make changes to, and review the solution that is being created before their very eyes.

Once you've achieved this level of participation at the start of a project, the senior IT management will remain involved during the entire project because they will better understand what is being done and they will feel as though they have contributed to the solution.

Chapter 2

Secrets Revealed:
Where Is All Of That IT $$$ Going?

Chapter 2: Secrets Revealed:
Where Is All Of That IT $$$ Going?

Where's the money going? Everyone knows that spending on IT departments and projects has been going through the roof for the last 10 years or so. Umm, does anyone know if the company has been getting any benefit from all of this increased spending?

Blame all of this discussion on Nicholas Carr's article "IT Doesn't Matter Any More" in the Harvard Business Review back in 2003 in which he pointed out that IT resources and knowledge have become a commodity so no long term advantage can be provided by them.

Ouch! So how does this all play out? There are three points to consider:

A firm can gain a competitive advantage if it has valuable, rare, and costly to imitate IT resources.

If your IT resources are not all that special, but if you use them to realize the full potential of non-IT valuable, rare, and costly resources then you can have a source of competitive advantage.

In the best case, if you have valuable, rare, and costly to imitate IT resources and you use them to realize the potential of non-IT valuable, rare, and costly resources then you really have source of competitive advantage.

Take that Mr. Carr!

But wait a minute, every firm spends loads of money on IT, why do only some (Walmart, FedEx) get a clear advantage from the money that they spend? A team of researchers lead by Dr.

Gautam Ray talked with 104 insurance firms in order to get to the bottom of this question.

Here's what they found: the key to getting the most out of your IT investment is to make sure that you have what they call shared IT-Business understanding. This means that business line managers and IT managers have to have shared domain knowledge and a common understanding about a specific business process and how IT can help make things better.

This shared IT-Business knowledge can't be bought. It develops over time. Firms that have this knowledge are able to achieve superior customer service performance even though the IT tools that they are using are also available to their competition.

The study also showed that technical IT skills by themselves don't really provide any distinctive advantage (sorry that you worked so hard to get that certification). Oh, and more IT spending does nothing to boost customer service performance.

In the end it comes down to not how much you spend on IT, but rather how your IT resources are deployed in a manner that best meets your firm's needs. This is how IT provides a true competitive advantage.

Chapter 3

Alternate Reality Games: Games That CIOs Know How To Play

Chapter 3: Alternate Reality Games: Games That CIOs Know How To Play

As a CIO, you've got some challenges facing you. You're managing a diverse and potentially distributed work force of highly skilled and talented IT professionals. You need to find a way to keep them challenged, and yet at the same time enable them to find ways to work together. Have you considered Alternate Reality Games?

Leave The Real World – Visit An Alternate Reality

CIOs have been taught that most problems can be solved with the application of some math and a whole bunch of data. However, they quickly have learned that the real world is much more complex than that – there are a number of IT problems that can't be solved this way.

Jane McGonigal has been looking at big problems like this and she's got a solution for us: Alternate Reality Games (ARGs). ARGs are immersive games that provide a massively multi-player experience. What makes them unique (outside of their size) is that the game-play unfolds in the course of their players lives over time spans that can range from days, weeks, or even months. This isn't your father's Wii.

Tools Of The (Alternate Reality) Trade

Ok, I can hear you saying, so just how do you play one of these ARGs? Well, it turns out that you don't really play it – it plays you! You already probably have some hard-core gamers working in your IT department, so why not? The folks running the ARG show, known affectionately as "puppet masters" are in charge of distributing potentially thousands of pieces of information that contribute to telling the story of the ARG. These pieces for the puzzle can be distributed via websites set up for the game, email, cell phone text messages, online audio podcasts and videos, etc.

The players in the game don't play by themselves – there is no way that they could solve the puzzle if they did that. Instead, they need to collaborate in order to share and gain information. They do this by using social networking sites (Facebook, MySpace, etc.), wikis, chat rooms, and blogs to talk about what clues they have and what they might mean. This interaction forms the narrative of the game.

Sounds Like An Effort – Why Bother?

Welcome to the 21st Century. McGonigal points out that ARGs are an excellent way for companies (and IT teams) to master those difficult collaboration skills that CEOs (and CIOs) want them to learn. Two of the skills that can be developed that she points out are cooperation radar – the ability to identify who can best help you, and protovation – the ability to prototype and test solutions quickly.

Oh, and by the way: ARGs are a lot of fun for everyone that is involved. Although they may be working through a simulation of a business problem that your firm is facing, it doesn't seem that way – it feels like a game.

Final Thoughts

When a CIOs firm is faced with a BIG challenge that doesn't have an obvious solution, playing an ARG may be just what the CEO ordered. Although they are not easy to set up, an ARG may offer the best way to quickly test out different scenarios in real world circumstances.

Above and beyond the business benefits that ARGs offer, by using this innovative way to stimulate and engage your department you will have found a way to apply IT to enable the rest of the company to grow quicker, move faster, and do more.

Chapter 4

Is IT Alignment Sooo Last Year?

Chapter 4: Is IT Alignment Sooo Last Year?

Is it possible that the holy grail of IT, getting our act together with the rest of the business, is no longer what we should be working on? A survey that was done by the consulting firm Bain & Co. sure seems to be saying this.

Before anyone goes crazy on me, let's first make sure that we're all talking about the same thing here. Just what do we mean when we talking about alignment? It turns out that the best definition of IT alignment that I've come across comes from Brian Watson over at CIO Insight magazine who defines it as *"...synching up strategies [between IT and the business units]."*

Now here's the trick: there are a bunch of ways to do this. Sometimes the IT organization runs alongside of the business units, sometimes the IT organization works within the business units almost like a vital organ.

No matter which approach you take, business line managers and IT managers have to have shared domain knowledge and a common understanding about a specific business process and how IT can help make things better in order to be in alignment.

The damning bit of info that the Bain report revealed was that if your IT department is not effective, then all the alignment in the world isn't going to help your firm.

The Bain team defined an effective IT department as one that gets projects done on time and on budget. Their study showed that making an IT department effective was MORE important than getting it aligned with the rest of the business if you wanted to boost company growth and control IT spending.

What this means is that too many of us have been trying to walk before we can crawl. Making our IT shops effective is the first step, alignment is the second step. Now there's a plan that we can live with.

Chapter 5

Just What Is This "Alignment" Thing?

Chapter 5: Just What Is This "Alignment" Thing?

Once upon a time the Supreme Court justice Potter Stewart said that pornography is hard to define, but "I know it when I see it." In the world of IT it would appear as though alignment with the business side of the house is a lot like pornography in this sense – it's hard to define, but we're all pretty sure that we'd know it we saw it. A survey that was done by the consulting firm Bain & Co. sure seems to confirm this.

It's always a good idea to make sure that we're talking about the same thing before we get into a big flame war. It turns out that the best definition of IT alignment that I've come across comes from Brian Watson over at CIO Insight magazine who defines it as *"...synching up strategies [between IT and the business units]."*

The kids over at Bain have found that the two sides of the coin, IT and business, all too often misunderstand just what the concept of alignment is. Specifically, what a lot of companies try to do is to dole out IT resources to different business units and then they say "Ta-Da – we're aligned". They really should be syncing up their strategies.

Bain believes that making your IT department more effective is the correct first step before you go worrying about alignment. Effectiveness is defined as being excellence in process management and execution. Of course, you need to be able to make these repeatable and consistent. On the other hand, alignment means that IT and the business have a proactive relationship.

I've always looked at these two parts of making the business run more smoothly as being joined at the hip. Effectiveness is how things get done every day. Alignment is the direction that you are moving in. Both are needed to have a well-run IT department.

Chapter 6

Alignment 101: How To Do It

Chapter 6: Alignment 101: How To Do It

Achieving alignment between the business side of the house and IT is one of those things that everyone likes to talk about when they are putting together the goals for the upcoming year, and then nothing ever seems to get done about it.

A survey that was done by the consulting firm Bain & Co. may contain the reason why we never seem to make any progress on this: we've been trying to do the wrong thing. The Bain crew believes that IT departments must first become efficient, and then worry about becoming aligned with the business.

Now the trick here is that you can't just do one at a time. Karenann Terrell who is that CIO over at Baxter International says that *"There is a complexity to doing both, but that's the job."* Her point is that you can't wait to become 100% efficient before you start to work on the alignment thing.

Let's say that you get the efficiently thing up to a point where it's good enough, what then? Too often CIOs view alignment as being a situation where IT stands ready to do the bidding of whatever the rest of the business needs. That's not what the business wants. Instead, the business needs IT to participate in the strategic decision making process – help do the thinking for the rest of the business. Perhaps a better word here would be "integration".

Finally, the alignment of IT with the rest of the business needs to be supported from the CEO on down. Without top-level support, it's never going to succeed. Strong collaboration between the business and IT is what will make alignment work. Remember that alignment is a dynamic process and that it will always be changing along with your business.

Chapter 7

How IT Can Help Uncover New Products

Chapter 7: How IT Can Help Uncover New Products

"Alignment", "Innovation" – arrgh! Who in the world of IT is not sick of hearing these two words used over and over again? Yes we'd like to be able to help out the rest of the business, but our IT budgets are being slashed left and right. We don't have either the staff or the budget to launch a big new program to collect whatever data is needed in order to tell the company which direction it should go in. **Or do we?**

It is in the nature of any IT department to collect **data on our customers**. We already have disk pack after disk pack of historical data about everyone who ever showed even the slightest interest in one of our company's offerings let alone how much information we have on our existing customers.

In that data lies the secret to how IT departments can help the rest of the company **uncover new products**. Ranjay Gulati, James Oldroyd, and Phanish Puranam are three researchers who have been studying this problem and they've made some interesting discoveries.

Harrah's is an owner of several casinos. Their IT department has historically collected reams of data on their customers in order to support targeted direct mail campaigns and attempts to increase customer loyalty.

However, it was not until the IT department took a closer look at the data that they had already captured about their big spenders ("whales" in casino speak) that they realized that they had the answers that they needed in order to **redesign their casinos** in order to position games where they would get these customers to play even more.

The Royal Bank of Canada faced a problem – its consumer credit division needed to have more customers. The IT department went back and took a look at the **credit card applications that they had rejected** in the past. What they discovered is that many of these people had improved their credit scores since being rejected. This gave the bank a great set of potential card holders to go after.

Clearly all IT departments are sitting on more customer data than anyone ever believed. Now we just have to figure out how to **make that data work for us**. It turns out that there are three principles that provide the core for doing this correctly. We'll talk about them next time...

Chapter 8

Do You Have An IT Dictionary?

Chapter 8: Do You Have An IT Dictionary?

In IT we often get accused of willy-nilly making up new acronyms on the fly. In all honesty, yes we do do this sometimes. However, there is a more subtle word problem that has been creeping around the edges of IT for a long time that nobody's been brave enough to bring up: **we have no idea what we are saying**.

Ranjay Gulati, James Oldroyd, and Phanish Puranam are three researchers who have been studying this problem and they've made some interesting discoveries. Specifically, they've discovered that we all seem to THINK that we are talking about the same thing when in many cases we really aren't.

In most companies the IT department serves multiple business units or departments. In order to meet the needs of those internal customers, the IT department is always creating new and different ways to present the information that has been collected. However, since nobody talks to anyone else in the company, we've been creating **a million different ways** to present (and talk about) the same data.

What's been missing from IT's output is some sort of **dictionary**. We need to standardize how we talk about the company's data and how we describe the results of the processing that we do on that data.

Over at Best Buy, Robert Willett who is their CIO said that when he first showed up they had **400 to 500 different ways to measure things**. What this meant is that measurements done for one customer could not be interpreted by another customer so they had to do the processing all over again.

Robert spent over 10 months and drove his IT department to a point where they had single definitions for everything. It was only after this type of IT dictionary had been created that Best Buy started to **get some value** for all of its efforts.

Chapter 9

Hey IT – Forget ITIL, Say Hello To BDIM!

Chapter 9: Hey IT – Forget ITIL, Say Hello To BDIM!

The world of IT is changing once again, are you ready? We have evolved a great deal in the last thirty years and it looks like we're getting ready to make another great leap forward. This time around we have a name for what's going to happen and it's called **business-driven IT management (BDIM)**!

Anto Moura and Claudio Bartolini have been looking at how IT is managed and they've discovered that we're getting ready for another change. Back at the end of the 1980's IT management was all about tracking boxes and routers. This was the era of **IT infrastructure management**.

Stability and control were the key drivers behind this effort. IT acted as a technology provider – IT folks were technical experts and their goal was to **minimize down time**.

In the past few years this style of IT management has changed. Now IT looks less at the infrastructure and more at the end user. IT now practices what is called **IT Service Management** (ITSM). The thinking is that IT services use groups of IT infrastructure components to help corporate users (and customers) to do business with the firm.

Viewed this way, IT has become a service provider. The downfall of this is that IT is still viewed as being separate from the rest of the business. The rest of the business believes that IT is mainly concerned with expense control. This has caused one of the firm's greatest concerns to become the issue of **business-IT alignment**.

We've come up with a whole bunch of technical ways to keep track of how the IT infrastructure is performing in order to ensure that our services are **meeting their performance levels**.

These tools include quality of service (QoS), service level agreements (SLAs), and when you combine both of these you get service level objectives (SLOs).

The arrival of the **IT Infrastructure Library** (ITIL) set of best practice standards has provided a way to deliver IT governance which seeks to ensure that IT risks are mitigated, IT is aligned with the rest of the firm, and that the expected results are achieved.

The problem with all of this is that the best practices, such as ITIL, are very useful, but they just don't go far enough toward **providing concrete solutions**.

This has led to the creation of the business-driven IT management (BDIM) approach to IT management. The goal of BDIM is to move IT one step further and start to use a **full business perspective** to manage IT. This means that we would need to stop using technical metrics measured at the IT level.

This can get a bit difficult to grasp, so here are a few IT management questions posed in BDIM format:

- Of all the IT incidents that are occurring RIGHT NOW, which is impacting the business the most and thus should be worked on now?
- Which services should we invest in to improve business results?
- How many standby servers should we have for our e-commerce site?

Since I know some you may still be struggling, here is a formal definition of BDIM:

"BDIM is the application of a set of models, practices, techniques, and tools to map and to quantitatively evaluate interdependencies between business performance and IT

solutions – and using the quantified evaluation – to improve the IT solutions' quality of service and related business results"

BDIM is still in the development stages. Models have to be created, how it related to the ITIL processes will have to be worked out, and creating BDIM decision support related tools will have to be done. However, yet another IT management change is **almost upon us** – and its name is BDIM.

Chapter 10

What CIOs Need To Know About Performance Management

Chapter 10: What CIOs Need To Know About Performance Management

Unless you've been asleep for the past couple of years, you've probably had a chance to read about the **Business Intelligence (BI)** fad that seem to have taken over the IT market.

The basic idea is pretty simple: use an application to crunch all of that complicated data that you've been gathering and present a simple **dashboard** to the CEO or whomever is making decisions. If the light on the dashboard is **green**, then the business is doing well. If it's **red**, then he / she needs to make some changes. As with all such things in life, cool tools often turn out to have a downside.

It turns out that BI tools and the reports that they generate are IT centric. This means that the rest of the company agrees that they look cool, but they don't find them as useful as we would like them to. It turns out that what they'd really like to have is **performance management (PM) tools**.

Performance management is defined by business needs and it provides the business' decision makers with the data that they require in order to make the right moves in order to **execute the business' strategy**.

PM shows up in a bunch of different places inside of the company. You'll see it in the **budgeting & financial processes** (there it's called "corporate" or "financial" PM). You can also find it on the operational side of the house. This is where BI is used to get more insights into supply chains, sales, customer service, etc.

I guess the easiest way to communicate the difference is to point out that BI is often about **dashboards and scorecards**. BI has been based on things that can be collected and measured.

Where PM differs, is that it's based on where the company **WANTS to go**.

This means that PM tools have to be created by consolidating disparate data that is often stored in planning / budgeting spreadsheets. Then these planning activities and strategies then need to be transformed by both the business and IT into **scorecards** and **key performance indicators (KPI)**.

The thing that sets PM apart from BI is that the **information** that IT collects to support a PM process is tied to **a model or a framework** for measuring performance. In finance, this model is the company's budget. However, once you move outside of finance then IT and the business need to work together to create a budget that they can both live with.

Chapter 11

---

3 Ways To Bring Business And IT Together

Chapter 11: 3 Ways To Bring Business And IT Together

In the end, it all comes down to **execution**. No, not chopping heads off, but rather how you go about having your IT department perform the tasks that the business needs them to do. How hard could this possibly be?

What's The Goal?

The power term "alignment" is tossed around a lot these days. I think that it's gotten used so much that a lot of us have forgotten just exactly what it means. In its simplest form, when a company is truly aligned then it is able to **manage both its business and its technology together**.

As simple as this may seem, too few companies are able to achieve this goal. **The reasons are many**: differing personalities, budgets that are unrelated, lack of accountability for business results, etc.

Fredric Fishman has spent some time thinking about this and he's come to the realization that in order for a company to commit to managing both its business and its technology together, then it needs to do three things well:

1. Provide a clear **vision** for the organization
2. Create a well-defined **roadmap** that shows how to get to the future
3. **Measure** outcomes against predefined criteria

One Strategy For Both Business And Technology

If you have any hopes of bringing your business and technology activities together, then you're going to have to make sure that the firm has a living **business strategy**. The world changes and your business strategy needs to be able to change with it. One way to accomplish this is to implement processes that will allow feedback on the business strategy to be collected and used to make adjustments.

The next step is to make sure that everyone understand just exactly how technology is going to be used to achieve each one of your **business objectives**. Finally, don't just hope for the best – make sure that you have criteria in place to judge success before you start any IT project.

Strategic Imperative: Talk & Spend

A company's goals are no good if nobody knows about them. Make sure that any planned investment in technology has a **direct link** to a business objective. This kind of decision making won't happen overnight. You're going to have to take the time to create internal processes that will allow your staff to learn how to make the correct investment decisions.

Once again, good **communication** is at the heart of any well run organization. You need to make sure that EVERYONE knows what the expected outcomes are and what the expected business results are. This will establish a sense of ownership and will make sure that everyone has "skin in the game".

Measure, Measure, Measure

The best IT programs in the world don't amount for much if you can't determine what their impact was. You need to **monitor the outcomes** of each IT investment decision so that your decision making process just keeps getting better.

This is where IT folks can really shine: collect those metrics, stats, and usage data and use these numbers to measure impacts and report results.

Final Thoughts

As you can see, the steps that we need to take to align technology and business are pretty straightforward. The challenge is that this calls out not for a technology solution, but rather for **a human-to-human solution**. Within IT we're great at writing code and hooking up new systems, now we just have to do a better job of talking and communicating with the rest of the company.

Chapter 12

IT Value: How To Measure The Revenue Of IT

Chapter 12: IT Value: How To Measure The Revenue Of IT

What would you say is the biggest challenge that CIOs are facing today? There are a lot of possibilities to choose from, but if I had to put my money on just one issue, I'd choose the fact that all that today's CIOs seem to get a chance to talk about is **costs**.

What's missing here is a way for CIOs to communicate in a company-wide manner just **how much value** the investments that the company is making in IT are returning – the revenue of IT if you will. HP's CIO Randy Mott has been facing this problem and he's come up with a solution to it.

Chris Murphy over at InformationWeek had a chance to sit down with Randy and ask some questions about how he's gone about communicating the **value of IT in his company**.

At HP, the IT teams attempt to put **a measurable value on the work that they do**. In short, it's the sum of the tangible (hard dollar) and intangible benefits that each IT project delivers in the 12 months just after full implementation is complete.

Randy believes that IT has always produced a revenue; however, we've been doing a **poor job of capturing the value** of what we do. The correct way is to report on the value of an IT project in such a way that it can be presented to the CFO / CEO / executive committee and have the numbers stand up.

How did HP pull this off? Simple – pre-planning. Before any project starts at HP, a complete **cost-benefit analysis** is performed and agreed to by both business unit leaders and finance. This means that the numbers are finance numbers – not IT numbers – and so they have credibility with the rest of the business.

So there you go – it is possible to measure the "revenue of IT". It just takes **commitment** from both inside and outside of the IT department.

It's from the forge of failure that the steel of success is formed.

Hard Work Does Not Guarantee Success, But Success Does Not Happen Without Hard Work.

- Dr. Jim Anderson

Create IT Departments That Are Productive And A Valuable Asset To The Rest Of The Company !

Dr. Jim Anderson is available to provide training and coaching on the topics that are the most important to people who have to manage IT departments: how can I build a productive IT department (and keep it together) while at the same time providing the rest of the company with the IT services that they need?

Dr. Anderson believes that in order to both learn and remember what he says, speakers need to laugh. Each one of his speeches is full of fun and humor so that what he says "sticks" with everyone.

Dr. Anderson's CIO Skills Training Includes:

1. How to identify and attract the right type of IT workers to your IT department.
2. How to build relationships with the company's senior management in order to get the support that you need?
3. How to stay on top of changing technology and security issues so that you never get surprised?

Dr. Jim Anderson works with over 100 customers per year. To invite Dr. Anderson to work with you, contact him at:

Phone: 813-418-6970 or
Email: jim@BlueElephantConsulting.com

Blue
Elephant
Consulting

Speaking.   Negotiating.   Managing.   Marketing.

Photo Credits:

Chapter 10 - www.twin-loc.fr
https://www.flickr.com/photos/xavier33300/

Chapter 11 - Nicolas Winspeare
https://www.flickr.com/photos/nwinspeare/

Chapter 12 - Open Knowledge
https://www.flickr.com/photos/okfn/

Other Books By The Author

Product Management

- How Product Managers Can Sell More Of Their Product: Tips & Techniques For Product Managers To Better Understand How To Sell Their Product

- How Product Managers Can Sell More Of Their Product: Tips & Techniques For Product Managers To Better Understand How To Sell Their Product

- How To Create A Successful Product That Customers Will Want: Techniques For Product Managers To Boost Product Sales And Increase Customer Satisfaction

- What Product Managers Need To Know About World-Class Product Development: How Product Managers Can Create Successful Products

- How Product Managers Can Learn To Understand Their Customers: Techniques For Product Managers To Better Understand What Their Customers Really Want

- Product Management Secrets: Techniques For Product Managers To Boost Product Sales And Increase Customer Satisfaction

- Product Development Lessons For Product Managers: How Product Managers Can Create Successful Products

- Customer Lessons For Product Managers: Techniques For Product Managers To Better Understand What Their Customers Really Want

- Product Failure Lessons For Product Managers: Examples Of Products That Have Failed For Product Managers To Learn From

- Communication Skills For Product Managers: The Communication Skills That Product Managers Need To Know How To Use In Order To Have A Successful Product

- How To Have A Successful Product Manager Career: The Things That You Need To Be Doing TODAY In Order To Have A Successful Product Manager Career

- Product Manager Product Success: How to keep your product on track and make it become a success

Public Speaking

- Creating Speeches That Work: How To Create A Speech That Will Make Your Message Be Remembered Forever!

- How To Organize A Speech In Order To Make Your Point: How to put together a speech that will capture and hold your audience's attention

- Changing How You Speak To Overcome Your Fear Of Speaking: Change techniques that will transform a speech into a memorable event

- Delivering Excellence: How To Give Presentations That Make A Difference: Presentation techniques that will transform a speech into a memorable event

- Tools Speakers Need In Order To Give The Perfect Speech: What tools to use to create your next speech so that your message will be remembered forever!

- How To Create A Speech That Will Be Remembered

- Secrets To Organizing A Speech For Maximum Impact: How to put together a speech that will capture and hold your audience's attention

- How To Become A Better Speaker By Changing How You Speak: Change techniques that will transform a speech into a memorable event

- How To Give A Great Presentation: Presentation techniques that will transform a speech into a memorable event

- How To Rehearse In Order To Give The Perfect Speech: How to effectively rehearse your next speech to that your message be remembered forever!

- Secrets To Creating The Perfect Speech: How to create a speech that will make your message be remembered forever!

- Secrets To Organizing The Perfect Speech: How to organize the best speech of your life!

- Secrets To Planning The Perfect Speech: How to plan to give the best speech of your life

- How To Show What You Mean During A Presentation: How to use visual techniques to transform a speech into a memorable event

CIO Skills

- New IT Technology Issues Facing CIOs: How CIOs Can Stay On Top Of The Changes In The Technology That Powers The Company

- Keeping The Barbarians Out: How CIOs Can Secure Their Department and Company: Tips And Techniques For CIOs To Use In Order To Secure Both Their IT Department And Their Company

- What CIOs Need To Know In Order To Successfully Manage An IT Department: Decision Making Skills That Every CIO Needs To Have In Order To Be Able To Make The Right Choices

- Becoming A Powerful And Effective Leader: Tips And Techniques That IT Managers Can Use In Order To Develop Leadership Skills

- CIO Secrets For Growing Innovation: Tips And Techniques For CIOs To Use In Order To Make Innovation Happen In Their IT Department

- Your Success As A CIO Depends On How Well You Communicate: Tips And Techniques For CIOs To Use In Order To Become Better Communicators

- What CIOs Need To Know About Working With Partners: Techniques For CIOs To Use In Order To

Be Able To Successfully Work With Partners

- Critical CIO Management Skills: Decision Making Skills That Every CIO Needs To Have In Order To Be Able To Make The Right Choices

- How CIOs Can Make Innovation Happen: Tips And Techniques For CIOs To Use In Order To Make Innovation Happen In Their IT Department

- CIO Communication Skills Secrets: Tips And Techniques For CIOs To Use In Order To Become Better Communicators

- Managing Your CIO Career: Steps That CIOs Have To Take In Order To Have A Long And Successful Career

- CIO Business Skills: How CIOs can work effectively with the rest of the company!

IT Manager Skills

- How IT Managers Can Use New Technology To Meet Today's IT Challenges: Technologies That IT Managers Can Use In Order to Make Their Teams More Productive

- How To Build High Performance IT Teams: Tips And Techniques That IT Managers Can Use In Order To Develop Productive Teams

- Save Yourself, Save Your Job – How To Manage Your IT Career: Secrets That IT Managers Can Use In Order To Have A Successful Career

- Growing Your CIO Career: How CIOs Can Work With The Entire Company In Order To Be Successful

- How IT Managers Can Make Innovation Happen: Tips And Techniques For IT Managers To Use In Order To Make Innovation Happen In Their Teams

- Staffing Skills IT Managers Must Have: Tips And Techniques That IT Managers Can Use In Order To Correctly Staff Their Teams

- Secrets Of Effective Leadership For IT Managers: Tips And Techniques That IT Managers Can Use In Order To Develop Leadership Skills

- IT Manager Career Secrets: Tips And Techniques That IT Managers Can Use In Order To Have A Successful Career

- IT Manager Budgeting Skills: How IT Managers Can Request, Manage, Use, And Track Their Funding

- Secrets Of Managing Budgets: What IT Managers Need To Know In Order To Understand How Their Company Uses Money

Negotiating

- Getting What You Want In A Negotiation By Learning How To Signal: How To Develop The Skill Of Effective Signaling In A Negotiation In Order To Get The Best Possible Outcome

- Exploring How To Get The Deal That You Want In A Negotiation: How To Develop The Skill Of Exploring What Is Possible In A Negotiation In Order To Reach The Best Possible Deal

- Use The Power Of Arguing To Win Your Next Negotiation: How To Develop The Skill Of Effective Arguing In A Negotiation In Order To Get The Best Possible Outcome

- Learn How To Signal In Your Next Negotiation: How To Develop The Skill Of Effective Signaling In A Negotiation In Order To Get The Best Possible Outcome

- Learn The Skill Of Exploring In A Negotiation: How To Develop The Skill Of Exploring What Is Possible In A Negotiation In Order To Reach The Best Possible Deal

- Learn How To Argue In Your Next Negotiation: How To Develop The Skill Of Effective Arguing In A Negotiation In Order To Get The Best Possible Outcome|

- How To Open Your Next Negotiation: How To Start A Negotiation In Order To Get The Best Possible Outcome

- Preparing For Your Next Negotiation: What You Need To Do BEFORE A Negotiation Starts In Order To Get The Best Possible Deal

- Learn How To Package Trades In Your Next Negotiation

- All Good Things Come To An End: How To Close A Negotiation - How To Develop The Skill Of Closing In Order To Get The Best Possible Outcome From A Negotiation

- Take No Prisoners In Your Next Negotiation: How To Start A Negotiation In Order To Get The Best Possible Outcome

Miscellaneous

- How To Heal A Broken Leg – Fast!: Understanding how to deal with a broken leg in order to start walking again quickly

- How Software Defined Networking (SDN) Is Going To Change Your World Forever: The Revolution In Network Design And How It Affects You

- The Power Of Virtualization: How It Affects Memory, Servers, and Storage: The Revolution In Creating Virtual Devices And How It Affects You

- The Internet-Enabled Successful School District Superintendent: How To Use The Internet To Boost Parental Involvement In Your Schools

- Power Distribution Unit (PDU) Secrets: What Everyone Who Works In A Data Center Needs To Know!

- Making The Jump: How To Land Your Dream Job When You Get Out Of College!

- How To Use The Internet To Create Successful Students And Involved Parents

How CIOs Can Use Their Technical Skills To Help Their Company Solve Real-World Business Problems

This book has been written with one goal in mind – to show you how you use the great technical skills that you have to help your company solve the business problems that they are facing. Learn how to use what you know to help your company move faster and do more!

Let's Make Your CIO Career A Success!

What You'll Find Inside:

- **GETTING & KEEPING IT TOP MANAGEMENT'S ATTENTION**

- **WHAT CIOS NEED TO KNOW ABOUT PERFORMANCE MANAGEMENT**

- **3 WAYS TO BRING BUSINESS AND IT TOGETHER**

- **IT VALUE: HOW TO MEASURE THE REVENUE OF IT**

Dr. Jim Anderson brings his 25 years of real-world experience to this book. He's been a senior IT executive at some of the world's largest firms. He's going to show you what you need to do (and not do!) in order to make your CIO career a success!

www.ingramcontent.com/pod-product-compliance
Lightning Source LLC
Chambersburg PA
CBHW071803200526
45167CB00017B/1198